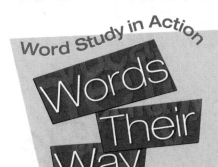

Word Study in Action

Words Their Way

Word Study Notebook

Donald R. Bear • Marcia Invernizzi • Francine Johnston

Contents

CELEBRATION PRESS

Pearson Learning Group

The following people have contributed to the development of this product:

Art and Design: Sherri Hieber-Day, Dorothea Fox, John Maddalone, David Mager, Judy Mahoney, Elbaliz Mendez, Dan Thomas

Editorial: Leslie Feierstone-Barna, Linette Mathewson, Tracey Randinelli

Inventory: Yvette Higgins

Marketing: Christine Fleming

Production/Manufacturing: Alan Dalgleish

Publishing Operations: Jennifer Van Der Heide

All photography © Pearson Education, Inc. (PEI) unless otherwise specifically noted.

Cover: © Mark Petersen/Stone/Getty Images; *kitten* © ZEFA Germany/Corbis Stock Market. **Interior:** *baby* © Don Mason/Corbis Stock Market; *barn* © Jeff Gnass/Corbis Stock Market; *bear* © Kennan Ward/Corbis Stock Market; *bed* © Brownie Harris/Corbis; *beg* © Jerry Young/DK Images; *bin* © Myrleen Ferguson Cate/PhotoEdit; *bug* Imagery; *camel* Four By Five/Superstock; *celery* © David Murray/DK Images; *cob* © David Murray and Jules Selmes/DK Images; *corn* © Roger Phillips/DK Images; *cow* © James Marshall/Corbis Stock Market ; *deer* Superstock; *duck* S. Nielsen/Imagery; *fin* Jack Grove/PhotoEdit; *fire* Mats Lindgren/Stone; *fish* Carmela Leszczynski/Animals Animals; *fog* © Donovan Reese/PhotoDisc/Getty Images, Inc.; *fox* Darrell Gulin/Stone; *gate* Elena Rooraid/PhotoEdit; *goat* © James Marshall/Corbis Stock Market; *goose* Bill Ivy/Stone; *hen* D. MacDonald/PhotoEdit; *hill* Superstock; *hit* © Jim Cummins/Taxi/Getty Images; *hog* © PhotoDisc, Inc.; *horse* Robert Maier/Animals Animals; *hut* Ralph A. Reinhold/Earth Scenes; *jet* Brian Parker/Tom Stack & Associates; *jig* © Stephanie Maze/Corbis; *jog* © Kevin Mallett/DK Images; *kangaroo* Fritz Prenzel/Stone; *kick* © Stephen Dunn/Allsport Photography/Getty Images; *kitchen* Dorey A. Sparre/Parker/Boon Productions for Silver Burdett Ginn; *kitten* © ZEFA Germany/Corbis Stock Market; *lion* David A. Northcott/Superstock; *lizard* Gail Shumway/FPG International; *mill* © Richard T. Nowitz/Corbis; *mix* © Dave King/DK Images; *moon* Superstock; *mouse* Gérard Lacz/Animals Animals; *mug* © Andy Crawford/DK Images; *mule* Robert Maier/Animals Animals; *nap* © SHOOT/PhotoLibrary.com; *nurse* © George W. Disario/Corbis Stock Market; *ox* © Ted Spiegel/Corbis; *parrot* Ron Kimball; *pig* © Don Mason/Corbis Stock Market; *pit* © Andy Crawford/DK Images; *quack* © Mark Petersen/Stone/Getty Images; *quiet* Dorey A. Sparre/Parker/Boon Productions for Silver Burdett Ginn; *rat* Breck P. Kent/Animals Animals; *road* Bill Bachmann/PhotoEdit; *rocket* Azure Computer & Photo Services/Earth Scenes; *roof* © Bo Zaunders/Corbis Stock Market; *rut* © Galen Rowell/Corbis; *sag* © Ric Ergenbright/Corbis; *seal* © Dan Guravich/Corbis; *ship* Superstock; *shop* © Rubberball Productions/Getty Images, Inc.; *stuffed toy* © DK Images; *tiger* Carmela Leszczynski/Animals Animals; *twin* © Ken Kaminesky/Corbis; *twins* © Ken Kaminesky/Corbis; *violin* Dennis Yankus/Superstock; *volcano* © Steve Kaufman/Peter Arnold, Inc.; *wag* © Carmela Leszcynski/Animals Animals/Earth Scenes; *wave* Warren Bolster/Stone; *wax* © Mike Dunning/DK Images; *web* J.C. Stevenson/Animals Animals; *wing* Superstock; *yard* Dorey A. Cardinale/Parker Boon Productions for Silver Burdett Ginn; *zebra* Patti Murray/Animals Animals; *zucchini* © Jules Selmes/DK Images.

COVER ART: Cameron Dalgleish, age 5; Brianna McCarthy, age 5; Angelica Wilson, age 5.

Printed in the United States of America

18 19 20 21 VO64 14 13 12 11 10

Celebration Press

Pearson Learning Group

1-800-321-3106

www.pearsonlearning.com

▲	⬤	◼

Draw two triangles, two circles, and two squares.

▲	●	■

Sort 1: Concept Sort Shapes

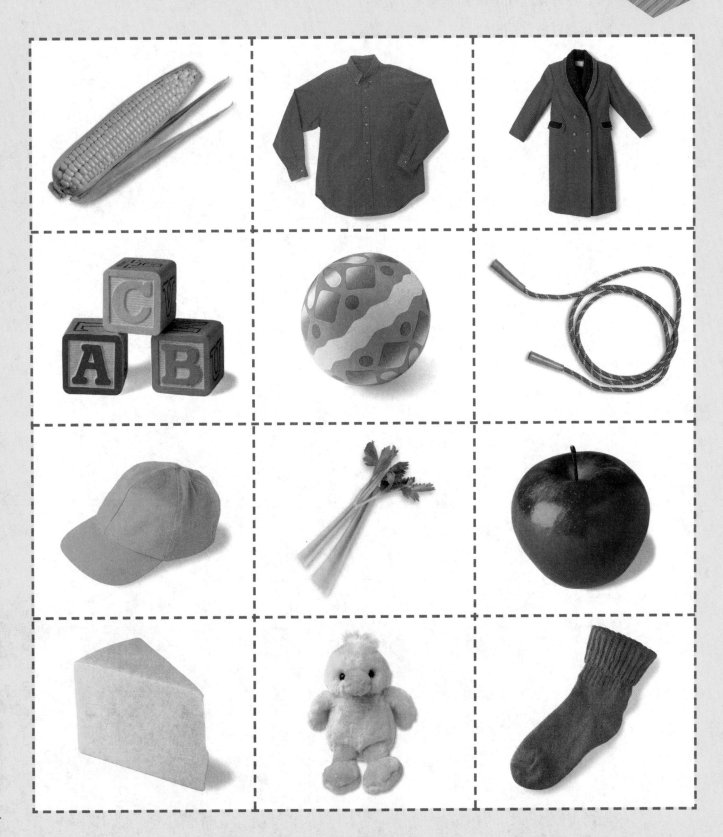

Sort 2: Concept Sort Food, Clothes, Toys ⑦

Draw two kinds of food, two kinds of clothes, and two toys.

Sort 2: Concept Sort Food, Clothes, Toys

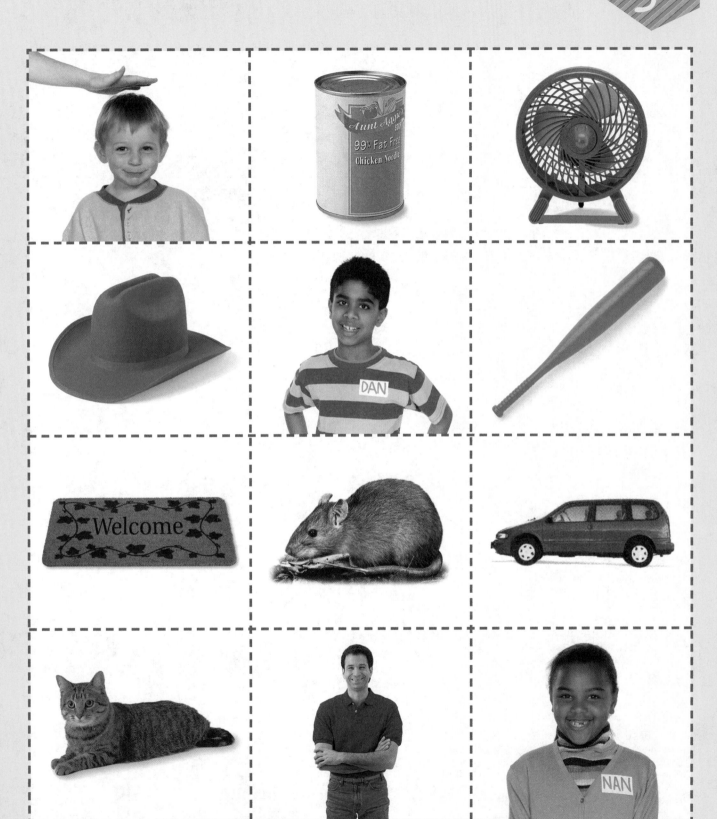

Rhyming Sort -at, -an

Sort 3: Rhyming Sort -at, -an (13)

Draw pictures of two things that rhyme with cat and two things that rhyme with pan.

Sort 3: Rhyming Sort -at, -an

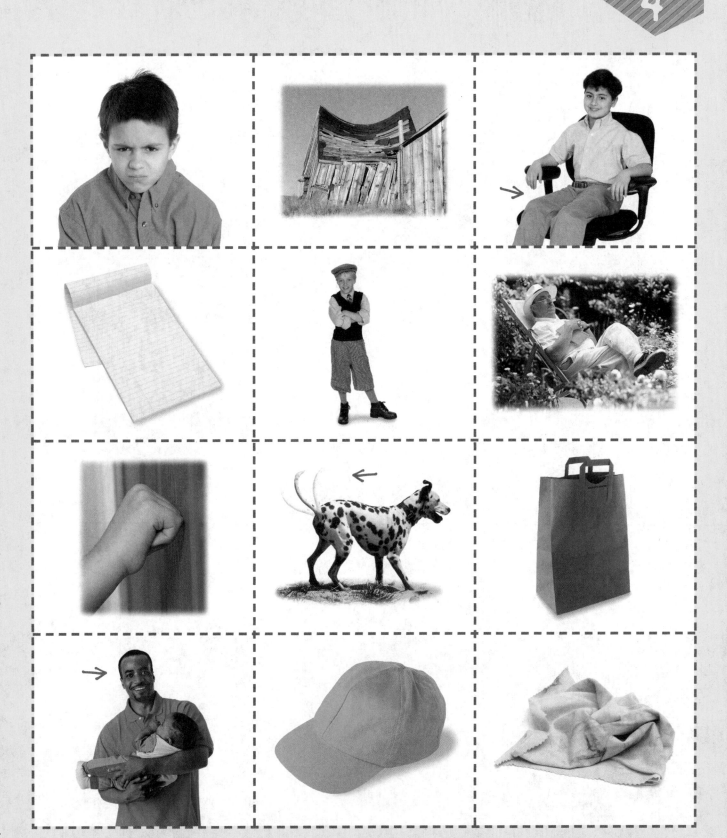

Draw pictures of two things that rhyme with sad, two things that rhyme with map, and two things that rhyme with tag.

Sort 4: Rhyming Sort -ad, -ap, -ag

Rhyming Sort -op, -ot, -og

Draw pictures of two things that rhyme with top, two things that rhyme with pot, and two things that rhyme with dog.

Sort 5: Rhyming Sort -op, -ot, -og

Sort 6: Rhyming Sort -et, -eg, -en   23

Draw pictures of two things that rhyme with jet, two things that rhyme with leg, and two things that rhyme with pen.

Sort 6: Rhyming Sort -et, -eg, -en

Sort 7: Rhyming Sort -ug, -ut, -un   (27)

Draw pictures of two things that rhyme with
bug, two things that rhyme with hut, and two
things that rhyme with bun.

Sort 7: Rhyming Sort -ug, -ut, -un

T	a	b	t
B	A	t	a
T	T	b	B
A	B	T	t
b	B	A	b
a	t	a	A

Tt				

Bb				

Aa				

Sort 8: Letter Recognition Aa, Bb, Tt (33)

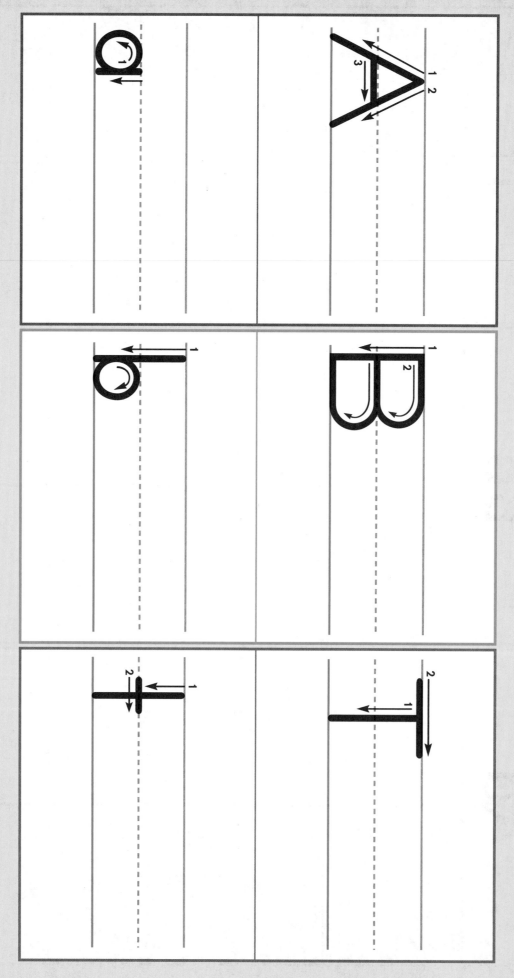

h	N	M	n
n	m	H	h
H	n	N	m
H	M	m	N
M	n	H	m
h	N	M	h

Hh

Nn

Mm

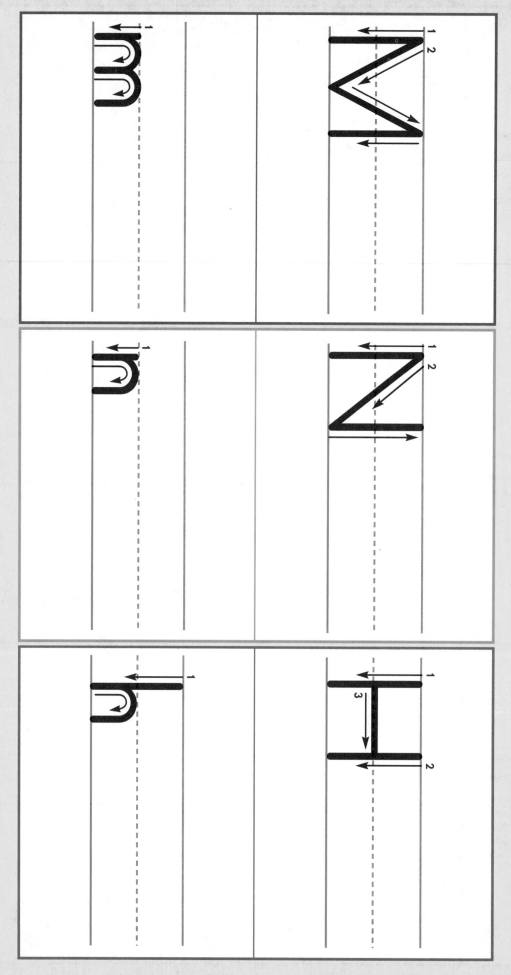

E	d	D	D
C	e	C	c
d	E	c	e
D	E	C	d
e	d	E	C
c	e	C	D

Ee				

Dd				

Cc				

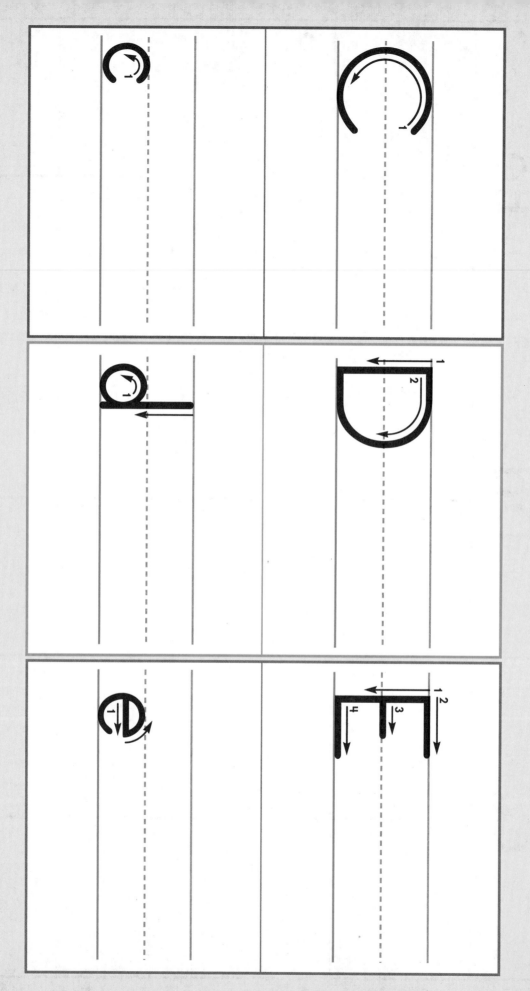

Sort 10: Letter Recognition Cc, Dd, Ee

F	g	E	e
E	e	F	f
e	g	f	G
G	E	f	E
f	g	G	F
G	g	F	e

Gg

Ff

Ee

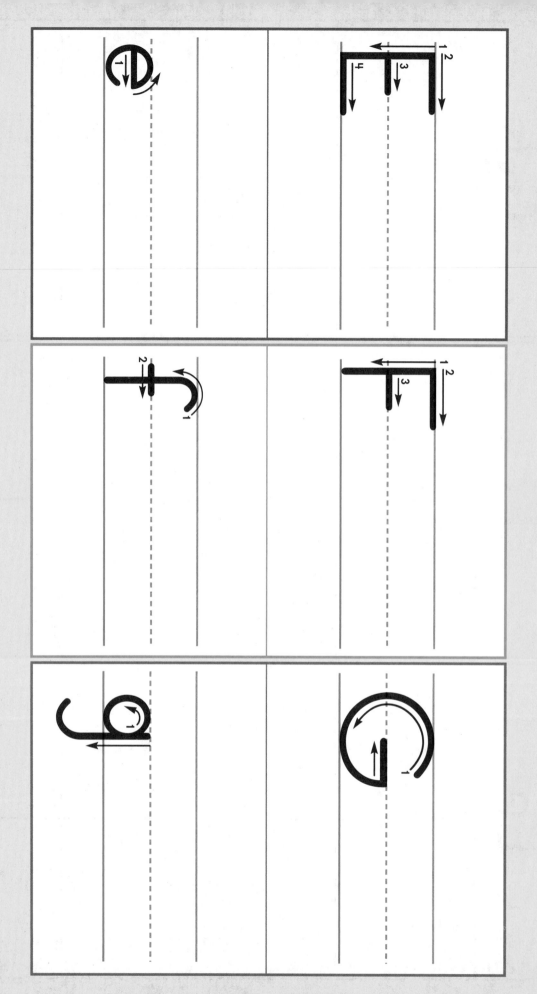

Sort 11: Letter Recognition Ee, Ff, Gg

K	j	J	K
K	I	i	j
k	I	J	J
i	j	k	I
i	J	K	i
k	j	I	k

Kk

Jj

Ii

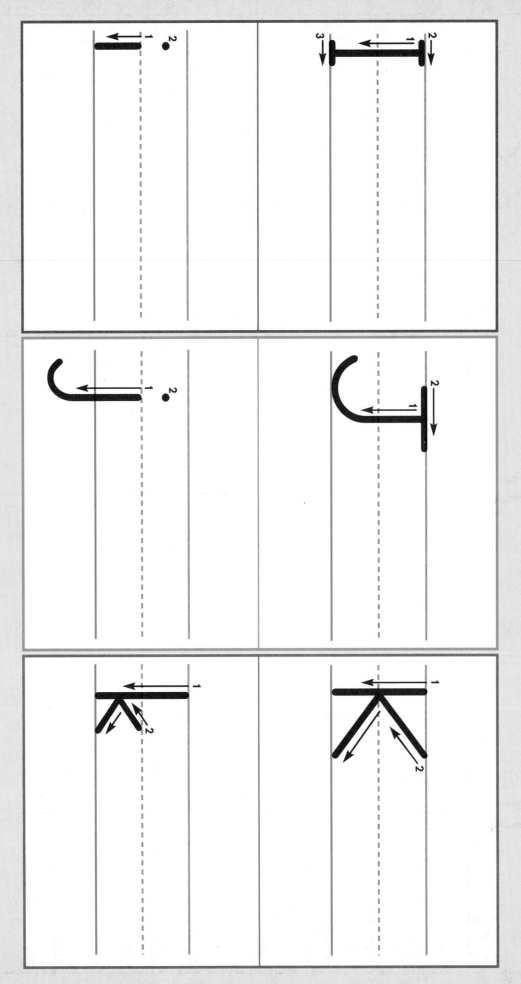

Sort 12: Letter Recognition Ii, Jj, Kk

P	L	P	l
P	L	P	R
R	l	L	P
r	R	P	P
R	l	r	L
l	r	P	r

Sort 13: Letter Recognition Ll, Pp, Rr ⑤1

Rr				

Pp				

Ll				

Sort 13: Letter Recognition Ll, Pp, Rr   (53)

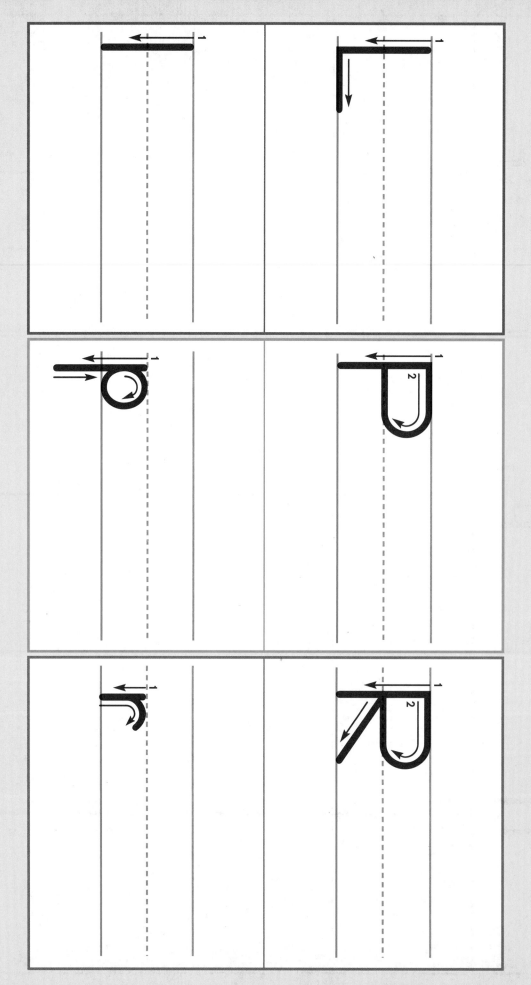

Sort 13: Letter Recognition Ll, Pp, Rr

S	Q	s	S
q	o	O	q
o	Q	S	O
Q	q	s	q
O	S	o	O
s	Q	o	s

Ss

Qq

Oo

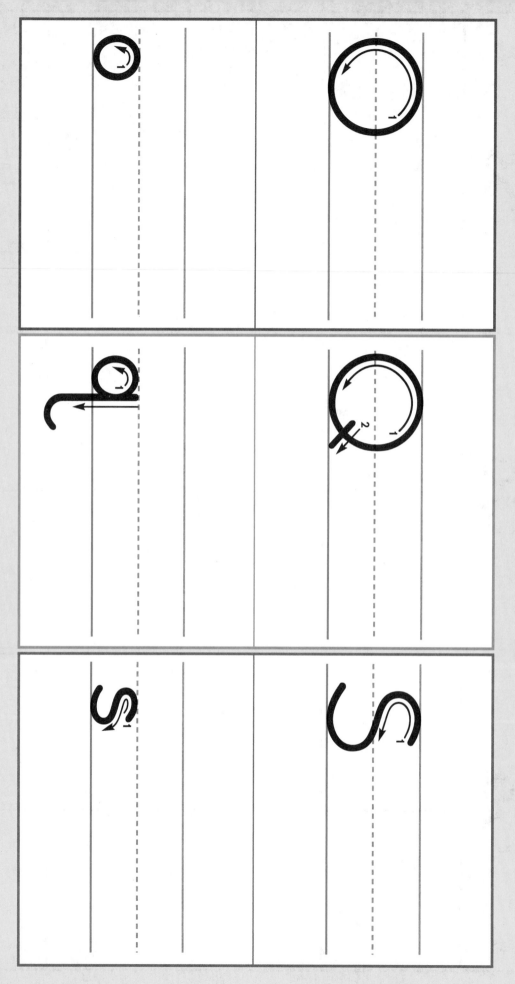

Say the name of each letter. Then print each letter on the lines.

58 Sort 14: Letter Recognition Oo, Qq, Ss

W	U	v	w
u	w	U	u
U	V	u	V
v	W	u	w
v	U	W	V
W	v	V	W

Ww

Vv

Uu

Sort 15: Letter Recognition Uu, Vv, Ww (61)

Say the name of each letter. Then print each letter on the lines.

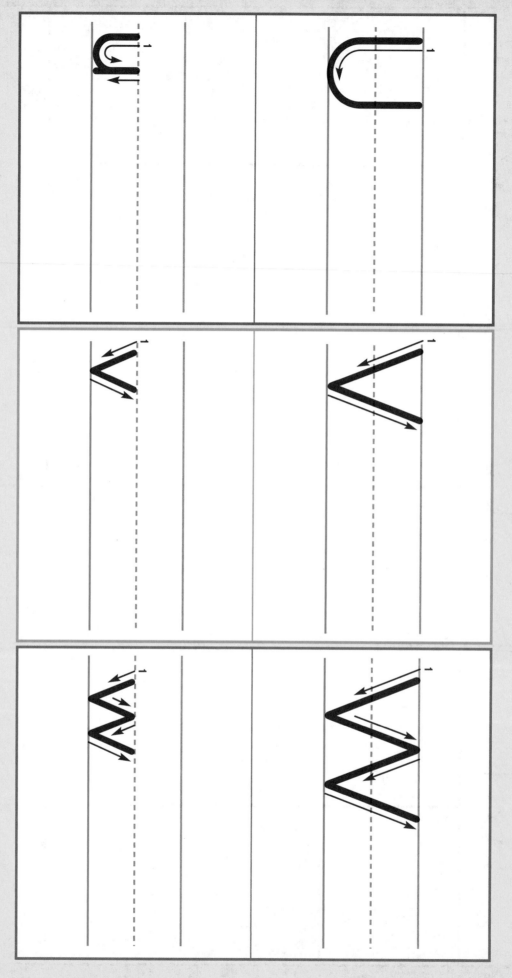

Sort 15: Letter Recognition Uu, Vv, Ww

y	Z	x	y
z	y	X	Z
x	Z	Y	X
Y	X	z	z
z	y	x	Y
X	Z	Y	X

Zz				

Yy				

Xx				

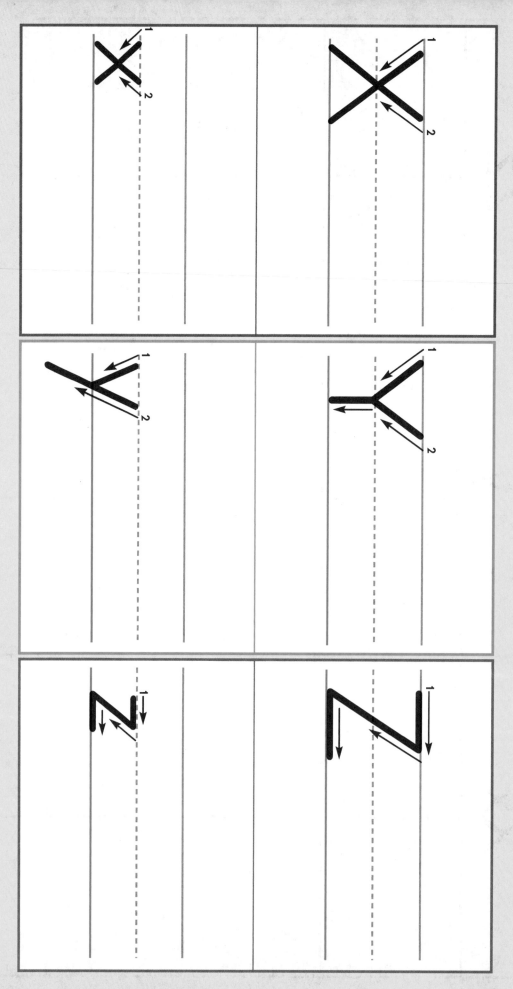

Sort 16: Letter Recognition Xx, Yy, Zz

Mm

Bb

Write Bb and Mm on the lines. Then draw pictures of two things that begin with those sounds.

Bb	Mm

Sort 17: Beginning Sounds b, m

Ss

Rr

Sort 18: Beginning Sounds r, s (73)

Write Rr and Ss on the lines. Then draw pictures of two things that begin with those sounds.

Rr	Ss

Sort 18: Beginning Sounds r, s

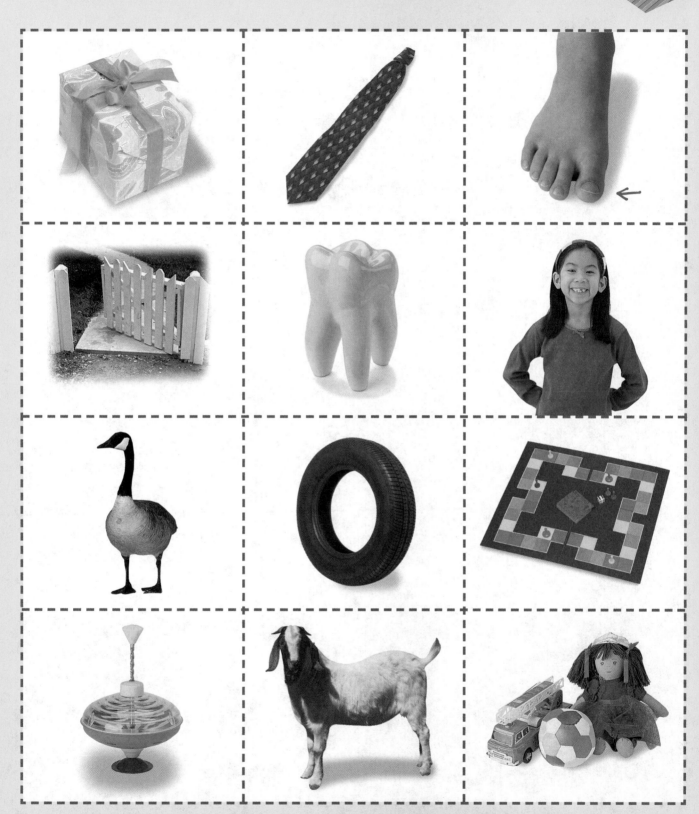

Gg

Tt

Write Tt and Gg on the lines. Then draw pictures
of two things that begin with those sounds.

Tt	Gg

Sort 19: Beginning Sounds t, g

Sort 20: Beginning Sounds n, p   79

Pp

Nn

Sort 20: Beginning Sounds n, p (81)

Write Nn and Pp on the lines. Then draw pictures of two things that begin with those sounds.

Nn	Pp

Sort 20: Beginning Sounds n, p

Hh

Cc

Write Cc and Hh on the lines. Then draw pictures of two things that begin with those sounds.

Cc	Hh

Sort 21: Beginning Sounds c, h

Dd

Ff

Write Ff and Dd on the lines. Then draw pictures of two things that begin with those sounds.

Ff	Dd

Sort 22: Beginning Sounds f, d

Kk

Ll

Write Ll and Kk on the lines. Then draw pictures of two things that begin with those sounds.

Ll	Kk

Jj	Ww	Qq

Write Jj, Ww, and Qq on the lines. Then draw pictures of two things that begin with those sounds.

Jj	Ww	Qq

Sort 24: Beginning Sounds j, w, q

Yy	Zz	Vv

Write Yy, Zz, and Vv on the lines. Then draw pictures of two things that begin with those sounds.

Yy	Zz	Vv

Sort 25: Beginning Sounds y, z, v

ax

bat

Sort 26: Ending Sounds t, x (105)

Write Tt and Xx on the lines. Then draw pictures of two things that end with those sounds.

bat	ax

Sort 26: Ending Sounds t, x

Word Families -at, -et

wet

vet

mat

cat

jet

rat

bat

net

pet

hat

Draw pictures of two things that end with -at and two things that end with -et. Write -at and -et below the matching pictures.

-at	-et
_____	_____
- - - - - - - - - - - -	- - - - - - - - - - - -
_____	_____
_____	_____
- - - - - - - - - - - -	- - - - - - - - - - - -
_____	_____

Sort 27: Word Families -at, -et

Word Families -an, -en

man	Ken	fan	can
men	ten	pan	pen

Sort 28: Word Families -an, -en (111)

hen

van

Sort 28: Word Families -an, -en (113)

Draw pictures of two things that end with -an and two things that end with -en. Write -an and -en below the matching pictures.

-an	-en

Word Families -ig, -og

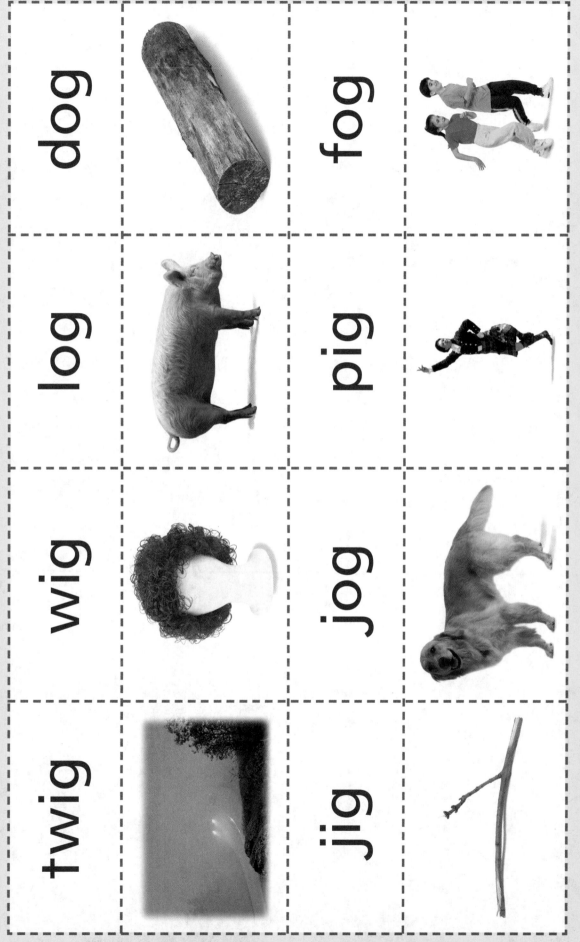

dog

fog

log

pig

wig

jog

twig

jig

frog

dig

Draw pictures of two things that end with -ig and two things that end with -og. Write -ig and -og below the matching pictures.

-ig	-og

Sort 29: Word Families -ig, -og

Word Families -in, -un

| sun | pin | twin | fun |
| bun | chin | bin | run |

Sort 30: Word Families -in, -un 119

sun

fin

Draw pictures of two things that end with -in and two things that end with -un. Write -in and -un below the matching pictures.

-in	-un

Sort 30: Word Families -in, -un

cat	net	cut	jet
met	nut	mat	rut
bat	rat	hut	wet

shut				

pet				

hat				

Sort 31: Word Families -at, -et, -ut (125)

Draw pictures of two things that end with -at, two things that end with -et, and two things that end with -ut. Write -at, -et, and -ut below the matching pictures.

-at	-et	-ut

fan

pan

twin

pen

men

bun

run

pin

sun	fin	hen	van

Sort 32: Word Families -an, -en, -in, -un (129)

Draw pictures of two things that end with -an, -en, -in, and -un.
Write -an, -en, -in, and -un below the matching pictures.

-an	-en	-in	-un

Sort 32: Word Families -an, -en, -in, -un

lip

rag

Say the name of each picture. Then write a or i to complete each name.

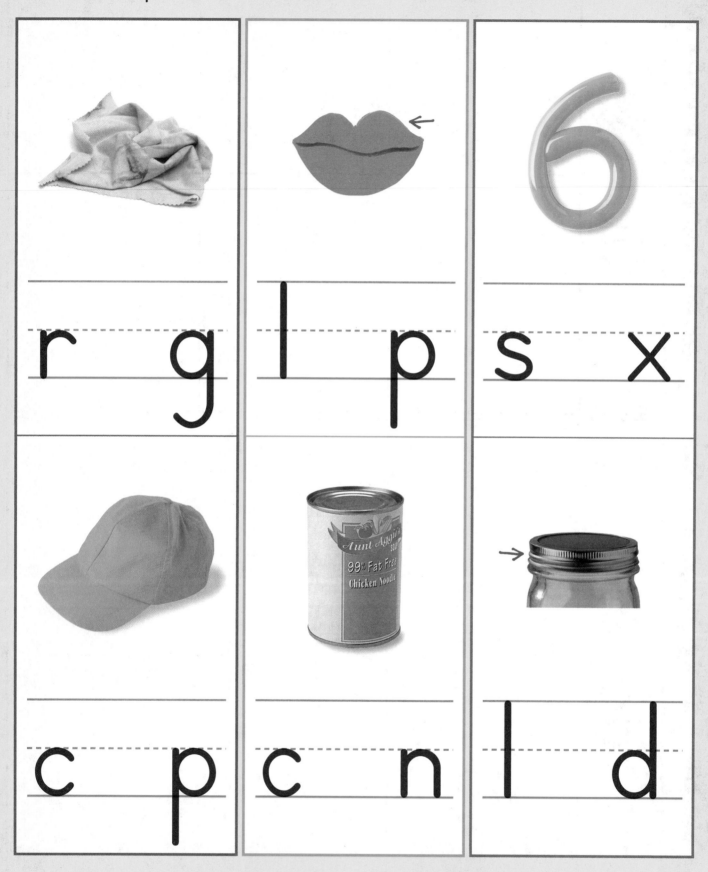

r g l p s x

c p c n l d

Short Vowels o, u

bus

cob

Say the name of each picture. Then write o or u
to complete each name.

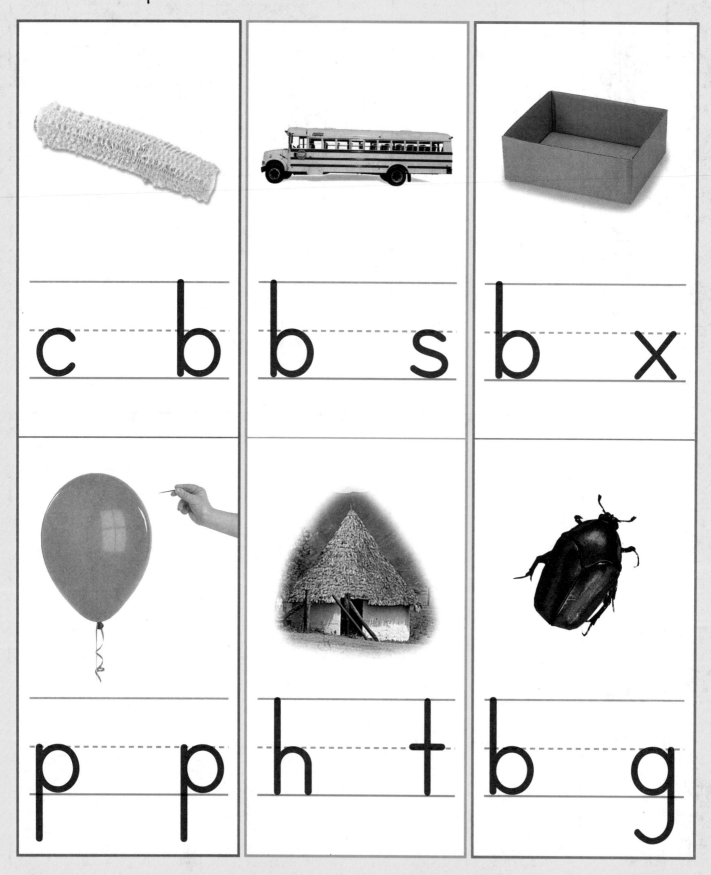

c b   b s   b x

p p   h t   b g

rag	wet	lip

Say the name of each picture. Then write a, e, or i to complete each name.

r g w t l p

m p b ll l d

Short Vowels a, e, i, o, u

Sort
36

Sort 36: Short Vowels a, e, i, o, u (143)

Words Their Way © Pearson Education, Inc./Celebration Press/Pearson Learning Group. All rights reserved.

Short Vowels a, e, i, o, u

bus	cob	lip	wet	rag

r g w t l p

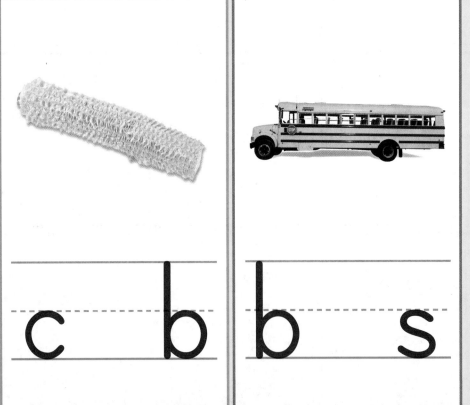

c b b s

Say the name of each picture. Circle the two pictures whose names rhyme.

1.

2.

3.

4.

5.

6.

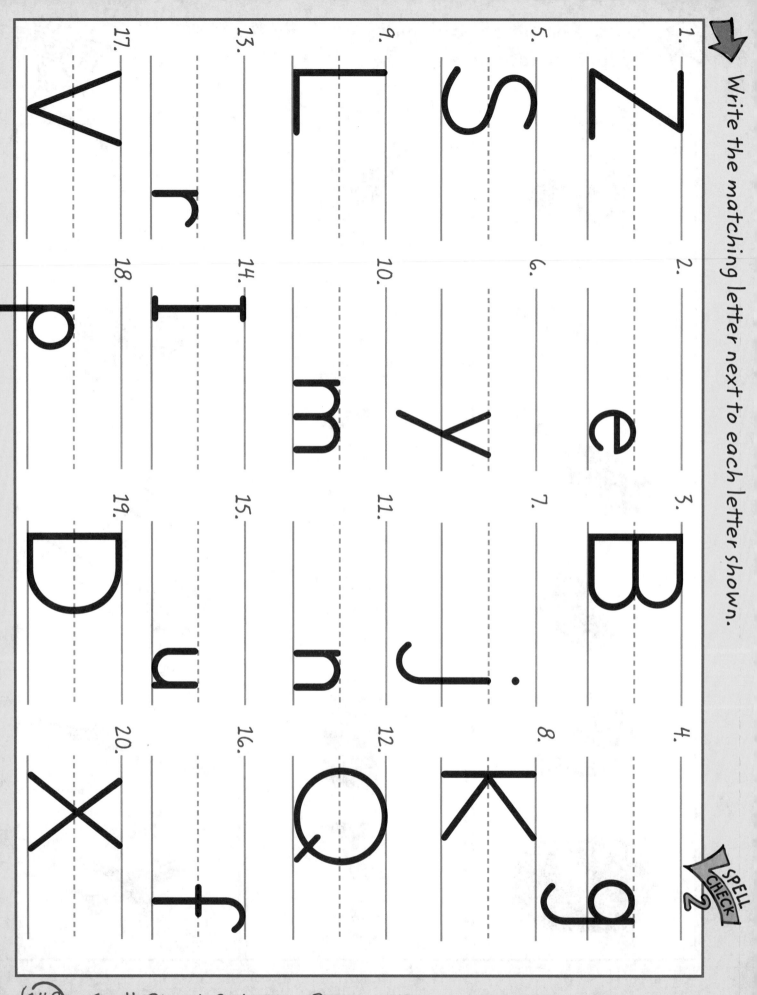

1. Z
2. e
3. B
4. g
5. S
6. y
7. j
8. K
9. L
10. m
11. n
12. Q
13. r
14. I
15. u
16. f
17. V
18. p
19. D
20. X

Name each picture. Write the letter that stands for each beginning sound.

1.	2.	3.	4.
_____	_____	_____	_____
- - - - - -	- - - - - -	- - - - - -	- - - - - -
_____	_____	_____	_____
5.	6.	7.	8.
_____	_____	_____	_____
- - - - - -	- - - - - -	- - - - - -	- - - - - -
_____	_____	_____	_____
9.	10.	11.	12.
_____	_____	_____	_____
- - - - - -	- - - - - -	- - - - - -	- - - - - -
_____	_____	_____	_____
13.	14.	15.	16.
_____	_____	_____	_____
- - - - - -	- - - - - -	- - - - - -	- - - - - -
_____	_____	_____	_____

Spell Check 3: Beginning Sounds   (149)

Say the name of each picture. Then write the name on the lines.

SPELL CHECK 4

1.	2.	3.
4.	5.	6.
7.	8.	9.
10.	11.	12.

Spell Check 4: Word Families

Say the name of each picture. Circle the name of the picture.

1. 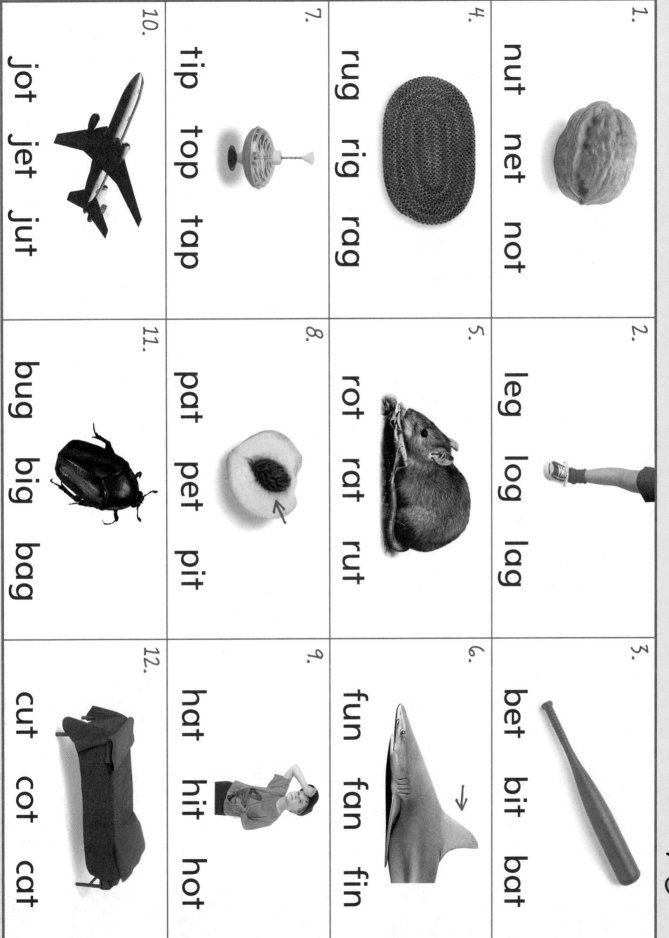nut net not	**2.** leg log lag	**3.** bet bit bat
4. rug rig rag	**5.** rot rat rut	**6.** fun fan fin
7. tip top tap	**8.** pat pet pit	**9.** hat hit hot
10. jot jet jut	**11.** bug big bag	**12.** cut cot cat

SPELL CHECK 5